Publisher'

Cop\

MW01503955

ISBN 978-0-578-08690-3

All scriptures, unless otherwise indicated, are taken from the New Living Translation Version of the Holy Bible.

Printed in the United State of America

Marquita L. Miller
Visit my website: www.faithpreneur.net
Email: info@faithpreneur.net

Photos by Trevor Logan
Please give credit of photos to Trevor Logan
(www.wix.com/focusedt/focused) (tcollects@yahoo.com)

Design Cover: Mario Loredo

Book Layout & Design: Next Level Enterprises
Website: www.nextlevelentonline.com

Acknowledgements

I want to Thank God for giving me the vision, knowledge and supernatural insight to write this book. This book has been inspired by the Word of God. Most of my knowledge has been received under the teaching and leadership of Pastor Steve & Donna Houpe of Harvest Church International. The 15 plus years of being taught the uncompromising Word of God by way of Sunday services, midweek services, conferences, trainings, women's meeting, encounters and one-on-one direction has provided me the foundation to birth this book. It is Harvest Church that provided me the push to start my own business at the age of 25 years old. It is Harvest Church that raised me to seek the face of God for revelation and release faith to unlock the door to the promises of God.

The releasing of faith brought me into the company of great people that have helped shape me into a successful Faith Based Entrepreneur. Entrepreneurship was never foreign to me since I was raised by a wonderful and strong entrepreneur, my father, James Muse. During my early years he taught me the importance of being the employer vs. the employee. He owned and operated a BBQ business the majority of my life; my elementary-college years. Those years birthed in me the desire of entrepreneurship. Those same years of childhood taught me the importance of helping others regardless of their level. I am the proud daughter of one of the most giving people that I know, Geneva Muse. The years of seeing her give, buy, help, and support total strangers without any hesitation taught me the principal of Sowing. I would like to think that today I am reaping the harvest of seed that she sowed in the lives of many people. The upbringing and influence of a traditional family sitting during the first 14 years of my life created strong family values.

That value for family is probably one of the reasons that I now have my own family and I consider being a wife and mother one of my greatest accomplishments. For those who know me, marrying a man that was an entrepreneur was not shocking to anyone. Tommie Miller, my husband, is a behind the scenes person but plays a major role in my success. He affords me the time to spend building a successful business that includes traveling and speaking engagements. He has provided me direction to make hard and critical decisions and he has been my encouragement to stay the course when things seem unstable. Tommie has been the nucleus for our family and he's also been the sounding board for thousands of serial entrepreneurial ideas. His new role has been to make my writing readable from the raw and uncut first draft. I am sure he has questioned within himself "what was my wife doing during grammar class?" That first draft team was my hubby, wonderful daughters, sister, administrative assistants, and a host of inner circle friends. I am sure that my writing coach & editor really appreciated this team.

I want to acknowledge the "Success Story Highlight Team" that trusted me to interview them. They let me call them numerous times, email them constantly, Facebook them incessantly, so that I could publish and print their stories for the world to be encouraged! I thank you for trusting the God in me! You can drop the restraining orders now, LOL.

Last but not least, I have to thank my mentors and friends for pushing me. I have to thank the connectionaire for sharing his connections. I have to thank my BFF for starting and finishing this process with me! Again, The Love of my Life Tommie Miller for sleeping with the lights on for several months!

Preface

Few people today are ignorant of the fact that our society is in the process of a radical change. In fact, things are changing so rapidly, that what once used to be surefire ways to save, invest and create financial security, now seem to be things of the past.

This book addresses these very serious issues. It's a comprehensive guide on how to win financially in turbulent times as a leader, CEO, Business man or woman, housewife, assembly worker, Pastor, consultant and even student. I know that this book will be as much of a treat for you as it was for me. It's a professional resource tool that's filled with insight, how-to, and permeated with faith to believe you can go to the next level.

Dr. Steve Houpe
Kansas City, MO

Foreword

I can personally relate to what Marquita Miller writes about in Faithpreneur. I operated my business for more than 25 years and know the value of having all the tools in place to operate a successful business. Having very strong family values and growing up in the church, I also know the value of seeking guidance from God in all decisions – business decisions should be no exception.

Faithpreneur begins with a discussion of "purpose" but not just any purpose but one's God-given purpose. How many people fail to think about the fact that God put each of us on earth for a purpose and it is our responsibility to find that purpose? The book uses examples, stories and exercises to emphasize points. The exercises are insightful and causes the reader to go internal and give serious thought to what they are doing and why. Interspersed in the book are stories told by business owners who share their experiences.

Adequate preparation and strong faith are both essential but one cannot succeed if isolated. Marquita gives exercises to help define and decide if establishing the types of relations can help grow businesses. Taking time to work through these exercises will shorten learning curves.

A dream without a plan is simply that – a dream. Faithpreneur provides a guide for turning dreams into action plans. Plans helps move from procrastination to putting visions on paper and then examining and re-examining for necessary changes. Putting something in writing moves it from a visual image to a concrete concept that makes it real.

The book does not paint a rosy picture of the life of an entrepreneur but deals with reality and "behind the scene" things that most people are not aware of when they see successful entrepreneurs. The nuts and bolts of carefully planning the business can lead to success.

This book is loaded with resources, examples, exercises and explanations that can help a start up or growing businesses. An important thing this book provides that most business books do not offer is the importance that faith and a connection to God plays in the success of businesses. Many people may think that the two are and should be separate. In today's business environment, there is an even greater need for more businesses – small, medium or large – to seek guidance on a spiritual level in making day-to-day decisions.

It is critical to seek that guidance and have faith that God will direct. Faith, however, does not replace the responsibility to properly prepare oneself. Proper preparation puts one in the position to accept God's blessings when they come.

Lillian Lambert

Author of The Road to Someplace Better:
From the Segregated South to Harvard Business School and Beyond

www.lillianlincolnlambert.com

Table of Contents

Introduction

1. DISCOVER PASSION FOR THE PURPOSE *(p.12)*
2. DETERMINE THE TIME *(p.18)*
3. ESTABLISH YOUR POWER TEAM *(p.22)*
4. DEVELOP THE ACTION PLAN *(p.30)*
5. SEASONS AND CYCLES *(p.36)*
6. THE CUSTOMER *(p.39)*
7. DESIGNATE THE PROPER ENTITY SELECTION *(p.43)*
8. OBTAIN FEDERAL, STATE AND LOCAL
   IDENTIFICATION NUMBERS *(p.49)*
9. CREATE AN ACCOUNTING PROCESS *(p.51)*
10. RESOLVE FUNDING REQUIREMENT
    AND OPTIONS *(p.56)*
11. RENDER UNTO CAESAR AND GOD THOSE THINGS
    THAT BELONG TO THEM *(p.60)*
12. THINK BIG! *(p.64)*

Resource Section
About the Author Section
Service of Five Star Tax & Business Solutions
Contact Information for Highlight Success Stories

Introduction

We probably can all remember being in elementary school and during the first semester being asked the question, "What do you want to be when you grow up?" The answer to that question is being examined years later by many and you have probably have reexamined it yourself. Have you asked yourself "What do I want to be when I grow up..." lately? Consider the following; of late people find themselves trapped in jobs that aren't providing fulfillment and companies have downsized. Some people have graduated with specific degrees but have been unable to find employment in their field of study. The SBA reported there were 29.6 million businesses as of 2008 and seven out of ten businesses last at least two (2) years but only half survive five (5) or more years. One thing that entrepreneurs have in common is that they are typically risk takers. The word Entrepreneur is defined as: <u>one who organizes, manages, and assumes the risk of business or enterprise</u>. Entrepreneurship is the driving force of our country's economy and the largest employer. It is the fastest way to financial freedom and renders one of the most rewarding feelings when managed properly. To obtain wealth some people sacrifice their families, health, and reputation. There are many people who are not willing to pay that cost. Following your dream and putting it all on the line can be risky business but have no fear, there is hope...

There is a resource available that is helping a certain group of people remove some of the risk of business. This resource is not a new age concept from a Silicon Valley start-up. The folk being helped are using two thousand year old principles to organize, manage, and operate businesses: These people are **Faithpreneurs**. A Faithpreneur is an individual that is an entrepreneur, a Christ-centered individual. This Christ-centered individual is serious about things of God. This person is willing to merge Godly and business principles. This person is willing to financially IMPACT the Kingdom of God.

This person's goal is to earn success with integrity, however, the difference between an Entrepreneur and a Faithpreneur is the process to the success.

Of the Sixty-six books in the Bible there lies numerous directions for favorable success of the Faithpreneur. The Bible outlines several positions that lend to being an entrepreneur: Vine growers, tax collectors, writers, weavers, tentmakers, physician, overseers, masons, messengers, lawyers, Inn keepers, instructors, landowners, fishermen, farmers, builders, bankers, treasurers, and oh I should not leave out the Carpenter. This book is designed to be a road map for the Faithpreneur and will provide 12 Faith-based steps to help create wealth and success. You can use your God-given purpose and your passion with business principles to impact the Kingdom. Provided in the back of the book is a resource section to allow you the referenced forms, recommended readings, and additional resources for research. Included are success stories highlights at the end of some of the chapters. The objective of the highlights is to motivate and assure that you know that there are real individuals like yourself that operate, manage, and guide their businesses by Godly principles. All of these business owners featured in this book are currently running their own companies.

All I ask of you is one thing; I need you to promise me that you will do this! Here is what you must do: TRY IT! Buy in to the fact that God is not interested in his people failing. Fear is not necessary. Also, follow the 12 Steps that are outlined in this book. Get active and also keep a pen, computer, or some note taking resource nearby. Tap in and you will win because God can't fail. Let's start the journey.

© Trevor Logan 2010

Good Morning

1. Discover Passion for the Purpose

" I know the plans I have for you, "says the LORD. "They are plans for
good and not for disaster, to give you a future and a hope. "
Jeremiah 29:11 (New Living Translation)

What is my purpose? What is the one thing that I would do for free if money was not an issue? Why was I born? What is the meaning of my life? If I only had one year to live then what would I spend my time doing? The answers to these questions reveal purpose.

While researching, I found an interesting definition of purpose. One dictionary translation indicated that purpose is the reason for which something exists or is done, made, or used. To identify the reason that something exists, is made, used or done, the most logical step would be to refer to the manufacturer of that item. Nobody knows a product better than the manufacturer. God is the original designer and creator of mankind; however, His first creation was NOT mankind. In Genesis 1:1 the Bible says that "God created the heavens and the earth." It was not until around verse twenty-six that God created mankind. That is a sure indication that man was created at a specific time with a specific purpose.

Let's think about this for a moment: A car manufacturer does not try to paint the car before the frame and body is put in place, right? Manufacturers have a specific process for the production of a product. God is the first creator to establish the order of the process. Rest assured that each individual person has been uniquely created for a specific purpose. We have been formed and fashioned for a specific reason in the mind of God. Just like no two people have the same DNA, no two people have the same exact purpose.

One of the most pressing needs of one's life is to tap into the hidden wealth of your purpose. The Book of Matthew gives us good insight to tapping into the "hidden wealth." In Matt 6:21 the word says "For where your treasure is there will your heart be also." If you can identify what has your heart (Passion) then you will reveal your treasure.

Many Faithpreneurs have given birth to the treasure. They are using their God given purpose (unique ability) and passion to start a business. At this point it is important to identify your purpose, especially if you are unaware of what it is. If you're not sure, finding out may require seeking direction from your manufacturer, self-examination, skills assessments and peer reviews. It is important to identify your purpose before you continue in this process. God has put inside each of us visions, dreams, plans and talents. The answer to WHY you were created will lead you to a business of purpose and fulfillment. Working outside of God's design can lead to failure and misdirection, which in turn can lead to strife and money chasing. The purpose identification process is the substance that will keep you moving forward during times when what you see is NOT what you perceived. It is the substance that will allow you to have faith for the next customer, deal, contract or engagement. Faith is the confident belief or trust in the truth of a trustworthy person, idea or thing. Everyone believes in something. We all take some beliefs for granted. When we realize and acknowledge that our purpose was God given then we know that we are not on our own. Once you are confident and sure of your aim then no one can talk you out of it.

You will realize that because of your unique God-given purpose you have no competition, however, you can still seek direction to sharpen your unique business position. You will know that you were formed and fashioned to do the business. There is assurance that you will know that you have insider information that gives you a competitive advantage. You will also know you have discernment that allows you to identify the true nature of people or situations. Using your God given purpose, Godly principles and a sound business system (plan) will allow you to create wealth and success.

"There are two great days in a person's life-the day we are born and the day we discover why"

William Barclay, author

Prayer: *Heavenly Father, In the name of Jesus, I pray that you would reveal or make clear my purpose to me. Your word says that you know the plans that you have for me and those plans are for my good. God reveal the details of those good plans. God I promise that I will boldly walk in my purpose. I was created for this purpose and accept the responsibility of my purpose. Amen*

Purpose Driven Reflection Exercise

The following exercise is designed to help you discover your purpose. Answer the questions below and review the connection that they will have.

Recall instances of great happiness. What where you doing?	
Recall a time that you have been occupied by an activity and lost track of time.	
Look up the meaning of your name, What does it mean?	
What are the things others tell you that you do very well?	
List your last great accomplishment.	
Ask someone close to you what qualities they admire most about you.	
What is your greatest strength?	
What things upset you when they're done to others?	
What positive role has a parent or parent figure said you would fulfill in your lifetime?	
Finish this sentence by writing the first things that come to mind: My purpose in life is …	

Success Story Highlight-The Marketing Lady

1. **Person Name: Tarsha Polk**
2. **Company Name: The Marketing Lady**
3. **Years In Business:7**
4. **Number of Employees: 1**

5. Business overview: The Marketing Lady™ is a firm that provides actionable strategies using innovative ideas and methods! We see above and beyond the norm and think outside the box by selecting the best ideas and approaches for efficiency and effectiveness! The firm has managed a broad range of successful public relations and marketing projects for corporate, small business, non-profit, and professional organizations. Experience includes budget development and tracking, creation and distribution of press releases, development of marketing / project plans and presentations. The firm's principal is Tarsha Polk. She has 16 years of experience in sales, marketing, coaching and training across a broad spectrum of industries. With her associates, the firm has a combined 45 years of experience in marketing communications.www.themarketinglady.com.

6. How does your business relate to your God given purpose? Some people do not know their purpose in life: It took me many years to hear what God was trying to tell me. Once I started to listen, it was clear that my purpose is to educate and empower entrepreneurs. So in my business, I fulfill my purpose by offering affordable business coaching, marketing consulting and training to individuals and firms that need the information and resources to grow one's business.

7. What is your passion? I am passionate about teaching entrepreneurship. Entrepreneurs build a stronger America by creating jobs, adding value to society and keep the economy going and growing. I strive to mentor an aspiring entrepreneur.

8. What biblical principle has been part of your business? 1 Corinthians 9:24-26. It talks about being in a race where the prize is eternal life. It tells us how to win the race by practicing self-control, to be intentional in every step and disciplining the body to win. Now that I know my God given purpose, I follow this principle to stay on track with achieving my goals.

9. What biblical principle would you encourage any entrepreneur to engage in as part of their business principles? Any business or personal decisions that I make, I run them pass God first. I ask for His will to be done and to guide me through the decision making process.

10. What business principles have worked that you feel has lead to your success: Philippians 3:12-14. This principle talks about pressing toward the goal. It reminds me that I am always on a journey to reach perfection; and look forward to the blessings Jesus Christ has intended for me.

11. What do you think you should have done more˚of or less of that would have made your road to success easier or shorter: I should have worried less, prayed more and told God exactly what I needed (Philippians 4:6).

We encourage you to contact this company for coaching, marketing consulting, and training to ind viduals and firms that need the information and resources to grow ones business. - www.themarketinglady.com

2. Determine the Time
A Time for Everything

[1] For everything there is a season,
A time for every activity under heaven.
[2] A time to be born and a time to die.
A time to plant and a time to harvest.
[3] A time to kill and a time to heal.
A time to tear down and a time to build up.
[4] A time to cry and a time to laugh.
A time to grieve and a time to dance.
[5] A time to scatter stones and a time to gather stones.
A time to embrace and a time to turn away.
[6] A time to search and a time to quit searching.
A time to keep and a time to throw away.
[7] A time to tear and a time to mend.
A time to be quiet and a time to speak.
[8] A time to love and a time to hate.
A time for war and a time for peace.

Ecclesiastes 3:1

In Chapter 1 we identified that there are processes and steps that must take place at the right time to have a successful product. The same holds true when you are giving birth to your treasure. Pregnancy is not a guarantee of fruitfulness. Unfortunately, we all know people that have had miscarriages, abortions and premature births. These things happen because of situations during those crucial times that lead to a sometimes devastating end result.

Our goal is to have fruitful businesses that will remain in operation. The Small Business Administration reported that 95% of businesses fail within 5 years. Instead of dwelling on why businesses fail, we are using tools of some of the successful 5%.

Determine if it's the time to plan or the time to plan and start. A person's financial, personal and family situations, available time, and amount of resources will determine whether it is time to plan or plan and start. If this is your season to plan, research your industry, review the market analysis, perfect your skills, obtain additional education, review the vision that God gave you, further define your unique selling position and obtain mentors. Even if this is your season to plan and start then realize that planning, research, and preparation almost always go first; everything begins with a plan.

2 Timothy 2:15 references that we should study to show ourselves approved unto God, a workman that need not be ashamed, rightly dividing the Word of Truth. Faithpreneurs must use that principle to have a successful business. Faith cannot be used as a backup plan for lack of planning or procrastination. The most important thing is to be approved by God. That approval happens when you say yes to God's plan for your life and act accordingly. You should never be ashamed to talk with someone about your vision because you have the facts (Truths) about your entrepreneurial endeavors. Also, the word of God tells us that we need to be ready in and out of season. That means that we should be prepared if we are in the planning only stage or if we are planning and launching our business.

Prayer: Heavenly Father, In the name of Jesus, I pray that you would reveal or make clear to me my season. Your word says that there is a time for every season. God I say not my will but your will be done. I know the vision is for an appointed time and I know that it will come to pass. I accept my season. Amen

Timing Assessment Questionnaire

The following questionnaire is designed to help you identify your season to bring forth your company. Answer the questions below and review the results to determine your season. The results will help to reveal if you are in a season to research, season to plan, season to be still or a season to start.

I have studied the top businesses in the industry I will be entering.	Yes or No
I have reviewed my credit report and made necessary adjustments.	Yes or No
I have reviewed my personal financial situation and feel that it is an appropriate time to move forward.	Yes or No
I feel that I have sufficient education in this field to be a workman unashamed.	Yes or No
I can clearly explain why my business can provide this product or service like no other company.	Yes or No
I have identified my current life schedule and it will allow me to give 110% to this entrepreneurial endeavor.	Yes or No
I have written the vision and made it clear to my immediate family. They are aware of how this vision will impact our family.	Yes or No
I feel that I have a support system to encourage me.	Yes or No
I am clear on my purpose and have a passion to finish what I will start.	Yes or No
I feel an undeniable unction that this is the TIME and SEASON to move.	Yes or No

© Trevor Logan 2010   FAMILY

3. Establish your Power Team

"As iron sharpens iron,
  so a friend sharpens a friend."

Proverbs 27:17

Developing your "Power Team" is a critical piece to your success. You want to identify the power team that will support you as you support them. Healthy relationships are balanced relationships. Relationships with no give and take are unbalanced. Individuals who take and never give can be time robbers; they are only interested in what is in it for them. As Faithpreneurs we have to acknowledge the principle of sowing and reaping. We do not want to confuse this with manipulation or giving with un-pure motives. Sowing is not about the person we are giving to; the truth is that we may not reap anything from the people we give to. I'm sure that you are wondering "How in the WORLD do I build a Power Team?" Don't be alarmed, scared or defeated. There are many ways to do it.

The business world hosts a lot of networking events and has even moved heavily into social networking. You can network daily without leaving your computer and you can connect with people from all over the world within a few key strokes. Facebook, LinkedIn, and Twitter have changed the rules, venue, and barriers of networking. A very encouraging theory that makes networking easier is the law called Six Degrees of Separation which suggests that everyone is at most six steps away from any other person that they desire to contact on Earth. We have the ability to connect with a lot of people. It is important to identify and never underestimate the people in your network. The people in your network should play a part in your success. We tend to meet lots of people. We have to realize that each person in our network has a circle of influence. The people in that circle of influence may be the key to unlocking resources, information, customers, contracts and favor.

Do not underestimate the power of your circle of influence. To grow your network remember power of the three R's: Recognize, Respect and Resource.

1. Recognize you have a network that can help you
2. Respect the people in your network
3. Resources are mutually beneficial for the network

My Pastor says that promotion happens at the speed of relationships. That means that relationship development is an important tool in establishing your Power Team. Many people have overlooked others that could have played a major role in the success of their business. Sometimes humans fail to respect the people in the network by overusing contacts for unimportant things. Then there are some that want to "Take" but never "Give" to the network. As a Faith Based Entrepreneur we should have no problem with giving value first. The gift of giving value first will open up and extend your benefit to networks. Most people can smell takers and needy people miles away. Faith and foolishness is a thin line, so do not jump the track. Nobody is going to do it all for you, however many people do not mind lending a hand to help others.

When the helper on your Power Team surfaces then you must be ready! Also know what to emphasize and when to use it. For example, many of us have taken marketing classes that teach us to know and spout off our elevator pitch/speech at any given moment. The elevator pitch/speech is good but what happens when you get off the elevator (this doesn't undermine the importance of the elevator pitch). No matter what... Be Ready! Be ready to tell people how you can help them and what you are looking for. Do not fall prey to the "Big Connection/Elephant" waiting game. Some people put the fate of their companies in meeting one person. Many people feel that as long as they can get a business card in the hand of this person it is all good. Business cards have been overly used in networking. The card should be exchanged after connections are made.   Just passing cards is wasting printed paper.

When you land the big meeting due to your networking, what happens next? First and foremost seeking God prior to the meeting or the event will save you time. The objective of networking is to expand relationships. Faithpreneurs must tap into the power of the Holy Spirit, even for networking. Answer this, how can people decide whom to meet or spend time in a conversation with? Have you ever been networking and felt that you got trapped in a conversation with the wrong person? You walked away from the event and felt that you wasted your time and missed other valuable relationships. You want to be able to speed the process up by asking God to direct you to the right person for that time.   Many of us have met people that we felt it was a "God thing". It can be a "God thing" every time if we have prayed and follow the leading of the Holy Spirit. Never put your future in the hands of a natural person.   God is bigger than any barrier or connection. Also, do not treat people like transactions. There is a person behind the position.

You will go so much further if you get to know the person not the position. When we focus on position and titles, that causes us to direct our attention upward. When we focus on people then it does not matter if it is upward or downward networking. Downward networking is looking at the person behind the position/title that appears to be less than attractive. It is typical for the average person to want to spend time with the CEO but the long term Janitor may have the connection you need too. Webster's definition of Janitor means the doorkeeper.

Many people are trying to get around gatekeepers but could go to the doorkeeper. God has a way of advancing those that should be the least in a big way. Be patient in developing your Power Team so you do not fill positions without relationships. The people on your team that are connected and truly care about your future will work hard and go further for your success.

With these new networking avenues, it is imperative that the Faithpreneur operates with discernment. The Bible says that the enemy is so deceptive that, if it were possible, he would deceive the very elect. Faithpreneurs must be sensitive to the leading of the Holy Spirit. The enemy only has three weapons: steal, kill, and destroy. The enemy will use people to release those weapons. We can't base our decision to do business with people on looks. Think about the companies and individuals who have gone from great wealth to bankruptcy or jail because they have been fooled. Let's face it, some of the ways we handle people are based upon our previous experience with others. The people that have helped or hurt us have helped to shape us. We have to base our decisions on discernment. It is important to understand the reason and purpose behind the relationships you have.

Expect to find people that will feel like they have partnered with you for success. Ecclesiastes 4:9 (NLT) says that two people are better than one for they help each other succeed. You can have Kingdom partnerships: The state of relationship between two or more individuals who have a conscious, calculated and consistent commitment to each other based on unshakeable convictions **to advance God's Kingdom.**

The bible shows us examples of Kingdom partnerships for success like; Ruth and Naomi, Jesus had twelve disciples that partnered with him; Moses was given Aaron, and God needs each of us. God is depending on us to help spread the gospel and restore humanity back to Christ. The success of your business will help to advance the Kingdom of God. You have the best player on your Power Team, and that is Jesus Christ. He will direct you and guide you because he needs you to win. Seek his guidance about the other players on your team. Ask the simple questions and expect direction.

• Why did I meet this person now?
o Example: I have had lunch at this restaurant for 5 years and never met the owner. Why am I meeting the owner now?
• Is this person God sent or a distraction?
• Is this person a connection for someone else in my circle of influence?
• What is this person NOT saying?
• What is my reason for wanting to connect with this person?
• Will this person push me closer to Christ or pull me away from Christ?
• Will I push this person away from Christ or pull them closer to Christ?
• Can I be "great people" to this person?
• Is this person "great people" to me?

Understanding relationships will help you not take people for granted or get taken for granted. Most relationships can be categorized by timeframe, purpose, and space.

Timeframe	Short Term	Long Term	Life Time
Purpose	Assignment/ Project/Task	Purpose Driven	Impartation
Space	Outer Court	Inner Court	Holy of Holies

Classifying our relationships is a tool that can be used to help you keep your interaction with individuals on the right page. You would not want to reveal the inner workings of your business to an individual that only has short-term place in your life. There are people you meet who impact your world so much it is hard to forget them. Some of these individuals may be your lifetime, impartation and you can safely allow them access to the most holy information. Many visions and businesses have been aborted or miscarried due to releasing information to the wrong person. You can enter into business deals with the wrong person and bring problems, issues, and unnecessary delays.

In business there are some key positions that will play a role in the success of your business. Successful businesses need an accountant, attorney, banker, insurance agent, vendors, referring agents, spiritual mentors, business mentors and mentees. The important thing is not the position but the people selected to fill those positions. The selection of those people plays a crucial part in unlocking the doors of knowledge, information and facts.

Business Connection Prayer: Heavenly father in the name of Jesus, direct my footsteps and path to the right people that mean me well. I call forth those people that are called to play a role in this chapter of my life. I release those relationships that are a hindrance to my purpose, plan and vision. Help me to be a good steward in all of my relationships.

Asset Inventory of Relationships Exercise

The following exercise is designed to help you identify the people for the position. Insert the name of the person that you feel is called to fulfill that role in your business endeavors.

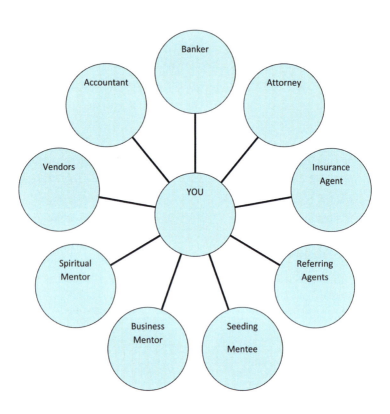

Success Story Highlight:
International Barber & Style College
1. Person Name: Uchendi Nwani
2. Company Name: International Barber & Style College
3. Years In Business: 12
4. Number of Employees: 11

5. Business overview: Create Future Barbers & Stylists

6. How does your business relate to your God given purpose?
Helping people develop their God given talent in the Hair Industry.

7. What is your passion? Helping people achieve their dreams in the hair industry.

8. What biblical principle would you encourage any entrepreneur to engage in as part of their business principle?
Matthew 25th chapter 14 – 32 verse. Using your talents. If you do not use your talents you will be cursed into poverty.

9. What business principle have worked that you feel has lead to your success? Having faith in God and never giving up.

10. What do you think you should have done more of or less of that would have made your road to success easier or shorter? Worked for a successful business in my field and then ventured into my own.

The global hair care market is forecasted to have a value of $47 million in 2014(Consumer Report). As you can see this is still a growing industry. We encourage you to contact this company if you have a dream of going into the Hair Industry. Also purchase a copy of his book Millionaire Ex-Convict.

www.1chin.com

4. Develop the Action Plan

"Work brings profit,
but mere talk leads to poverty!"

Proverbs 14:23

Developing a plan... this is the part that separates the talkers from the doers. We have all talked with people who constantly talk about all their aspirations. You walk away amazed at how resourceful they are, how talented they are or how smart they are. You wonder why they aren't further down the road, more successful, a multi-millionaire; they haven't produced a CD, started a business or created an award winning invention. We know these sharp people and you may be one of those sharp people.

Many people, including these sharp men and women, struggle with some sort of procrastination. Procrastination is the art of putting off, delaying or deferring an action to a later time. This is an art because it is typically a habitual action or way of thinking (collection of the habit). Procrastinators are not born they are made.

Let's look at some of the types of procrastinators

- Chronic procrastinators: This is a lifestyle for them.
- Optimist procrastinators: This is the " I work best under pres sure group."
- Thrill-seeking procrastinators: They love the rush of the dead line.
- Distraction procrastinators: They allow everything and anything to alter their day.
- Rebellious procrastinators: They just really do not want to do it and will put it off.

- Avoiding procrastinators: They have a fear of a negative outcome so delay the process.
- Indecisive procrastinators: They can never make up their mind so nothing gets done.

Many dreams, plans, and actions have been delayed because of people that fit neatly in the categories listed above. The good news is that we serve a God that can help us break any chain of bondage that we may face in life. The first step is to be truthful with ourselves and admit that we have a problem in this area. Secondly, it is imperative that you pray and ask God for help in this area of your life. The final (and most important) step after prayer is to change the behavior by creating a new habit. My Pastor, Dr. Steve Houpe, says that anything you can do consecutively for 21 days will become a habit. For the next 21 days write down the things that you have to accomplish for the day then make sure you do them ALL that day… no excuses. I can testify about this being the truth. The fact that you are reading this book is due to the result of this process to form new habits. It is important for us to tackle this section because the next set of instructions will be technical lessons that require you to do something!

The first step is to use the research and information collected in chapter two to develop a business plan or summary. As a business consultant I have visited with numerous business owners, both successful and struggling and here's a startling truth; 1 out of 5 clients I meet with have a plan. The business plan is a road map for you to shape and prove out your business concept. When I am teaching at a certain faith-based business school I like to refer to the business plan as a "Go/No Go form". For them to be accepted into the program they had to have a God-given vision. As an instructor, I am challenged with the task of helping them sharpen up the concept and strategy of how they get the desired end result. We say "Go/NO Go form" because until the student can see that the written plan can produce the desired fruit it is a NO Go. This can be a great process for seasoned business owners to revisit. Is the business producing the revenue to support the expenses? Is the business owner stressed out daily because of the results of business? Business owners should honestly evaluate the results or fruit of the business. If your business has not worked according to the initial business plan then perhaps it is time to restructure and re-evaluate. Has technology, regulations, or process changed in your industry? Do not let your business become obsolete. All of the changes can lead you to a more profitable way of doing business. Customers may stay with you from faithfulness or loyalty for a while but you may lose market shares for failure to update. Make it a practice to regularly assess the effectiveness of your product/ services. Your brand, concepts, or processes may have been a Go in 1998 but due to the way the world has changed and continues to change so rapidly, it's turned to a NO Go in 2012. Successful Entrepreneurs have to be able to make adjustments when things are not working. Faithpreneurs need to ask God to show them the unknown opportunities and make the change quickly. I have provided a sample "Go/NO Go form" and business plan outline in the resource section.

The next step is to create an Action Plan. This is a process I often use in my consulting practice. I notice that some of my clients have a great plan but no system for engaging it. What do I mean by that? This is the process of mapping out the required task to meet your desired goal in the next 30, 60 or 90 days. I like to think of it as backward planning or starting with the end in mind where planning is concerned. List the goal that you want to accomplish and what it will take to reach the goal; this is the stage for your daily to do list. If you get into the habit of listing goals then at the end of each day you should have movement. Don't get caught up in a trap that happens to many aspiring to be in business: please do not confuse busy with forward progression. You can be busy doing more of the same stuff that hasn't worked in the past. You can be busy doing more of the same stuff that has channeled you to this point in your life. Insanity is doing the same thing and expecting different results. If you do not like what you see then change what you are doing!

What is a word that has the ability to make adults as afraid as children who are scared of the dark? CHANGE! Change is a word that can make us uncomfortable. When we change where we play, how we play, and whom we play with everything is new. Those new opportunities can produce new results. Many people say that they want something different but are not willing to pay the price of being in uncharted territory. Change is uncomfortable but if you're willing to sacrifice that, you'll live the God designed life that goes beyond your wildest dreams. The new place may cost you friends and gain you enemies. God is not required to speak to others about something he is directing you to do. It may seem crazy to someone else but you have unexplainable peace. Make the change! As longs as you know that God is leading you to the change then you are in the best position. Ask the Lord to reveal to you the things you need to change in your life that are hindering growth.

Also, this is the step when you may need to engage some of your power team players. This should be a mentor, coach, or accountability partner that can help you get on the right track as you get started. I once heard a minister say that you have to put feet to your faith. Remember, you are a person of action and procrastination was eliminated from your life, in Jesus name!

Backward Planning Exercise
The following exercise is designed to help you...

How much money do you plan to make in your first year of business, if just starting up or next year if already an existing business?	
How many employees will you need to hire to hit this goal?	
If you sell a product, how many do you have to sell to make this revenue?	
If you provide a service, how many services do you need to provide to make this revenue?	

© Trevor Logan 2010

5. Seasons and Cycles

"that you may be sons of your Father in heaven. He causes his sun to rise on the evil and the good, and sends rain on the righteous and the unrighteous"

Matthew 5:45

Every business will experience expansion and contraction. These are the slow and fast periods you'll experience in business; the season and cycles of business are not predictable. We would all love to experience the growth cycle only. However, that may not be the case. You can do all the advertisement that you want to do, just realize that at some point you will experience a slowing of business. That slowing is only a problem if you have not properly prepared for that season. I know that this goes against the grain of most Faith Based individual. Let me provide evidence. Think about your personal financial situation five years ago. What did your situation look like?

Were you in business? Yes or No

What was your business revenue that year? _____

Were you employed? Yes or NO

What was your salary? _____

How much was in your retirement account? _____

How much did you have in a saving account? _____

How many customer did you have in business? _____

Now, let's advance and review those same questions based upon your current situation today. How much have things changed from five years ago? I am sure that things have improved or unfortunately gotten worst. Faith based individuals seem to think that God has forgotten about them if things are not advancing as planned. Sometimes those difficulties can create the perfect environment of total reliance on God. Those times somehow tend to push each of us closer to God. Those times allow us to know that without God that we are nothing.

The times when business is slow also allows us to see how our own decision-making, knowledge, and wisdom will never compare to the Master's plans. Also, these times often reveal things about the people around you. Some people are around you only when things are working well. Those times shake our tree and many things may fall. Those things that fall, change, or are removed need to be loosed at that season for advancement. I remember during the first six months of starting my business when I thought that I had missed God. People that said they would patronize me couldn't be found; customers that were supposed to pay didn't follow the plan. The vision that God showed me was not what I was experiencing. In fact, it looked like I was headed for destruction. That time revealed shallow friends and those times also humbled me.

Those times built my confident assurance that this would not be done by might, nor power but by the spirit of the Lord. I tried to end my personal mission of faithpreneurship and return to the workforce that I had exited, however, God allowed those doors to remain closed so that my mindset could be developed. I had to understand that "This is NOT that". This business would not be done according to my MBA training. This business would not be a success by the business worldview point; this business would only be done by renewing my mind. This would only happen by studying the Word of God and seeking the face of God for direction. I had to take authority over fear and disappointment.

I had to develop courage and expectation. I had to break the old patterns and develop new patterns.

What are some of the new patterns? Patterns of believing the Word of God despite what the situation looked like. I had to use my imagination to visualize success. I had to hear the phone ring before it started ringing off the hook. I had to see the customer waiting in line before they were waiting. You and I have been created in the image of God! The same God that created the heavens and the earth, that get's me excited. We have the creative ability to imagine what we desire to see. Another thing that gives me hope for you, is that we can build up our expectation for our desires in such a strong way, that it will attract everything we need to bring our visions to pass. Our desire has to be so strong that nothing but success is an option. We have to want it as bad as we want our next breath of air. If you are in a season that is less desirable, know that changing it starts with YOU. Change your season and cycle. Be strong and of good courage, meditate on the word and see yourself out of the season. Don't forget to listen to the direction of God during this season. That direction may reveal to you solutions that will change your situation overnight. Remember every day is a new DAY!

6. The Customer

"There is no lack, for my God supplies all my needs according to his riches"

Philippians 4:19

Some entrepreneurs think if you build it then they will come. Although "Field of Dreams" is a classic movie, that theory has proven to be a fail proof system. Businesses have opened and closed as a result of poor marketing. It goes hand-in-hand with the fact that a person is only a leader if someone is following. An organization is only a business if you have customers. Jesus was one of the greatest marketers. The Bible is considered the most published book of all time; it has sold an estimate of over 6 billion copies worldwide. Those numbers are very impressive so let's examine how he gained followers (customers).

Great crowds of people followed Jesus because of the miracles that he performed. Jesus' first miracle was turning water into wine. The water was what He had and the wine was the supplying of all my needs. As Faithpreneurs we have to take what we have and turn it into what we desire. If you have no clients then you need to allow others to see your work (Miracles) so you can gain customers (followers). Perhaps you have to volunteer your services or provide your product for free the first few times. You need to gain the reports of the benefits of your service and product.

Once you have proven satisfied customers then you may need to use them to gain more. To gain momentum for your business you must treat people right, especially when you're a new business. All you have is your reputation. If you want them to give you revenue and referrals then give them value.

The value comes when you provide them more than expected. Something I like to call "under-promising or giving face value and then over delivering." As a Faithpreneur your customer should notice that doing business with you yields more fruit. The fruit is yielded because you are praying for your customer. You are seeking God on their behavior and for you to have wisdom. They will not understand why you seem to have all the answers. At the same time, make sure you are careful not to get your prayer time confused with your work time. Your prayer time will be 90% behind the scenes. People are paying you to provide a service and are NOT expecting a Bible study every time they come to your business. There is that 10% of the time that the spirit of the Lord (NOT flesh) will lead you to pray with that person.

You will have to use your number one weapon to call in customers. The word of God says that life and death are in the power of your tongue. Your tongue can speak life into your businesses. Call the customer into your business by confessing their existence. You will want to confess often (even daily) that paying customers are coming from the north, south, east and the west. Before you get up in the morning thank God that your set angels have already been assigned to bring success to you on this day. Thank God for putting you on the hearts and minds of people. You will recognize the answer of prayer when people call you and say I had to get this done today, I was just thinking about you or I just told someone about your businesses. Yes, faith without work is dead. Make sure you are ready to work when they show up. Make sure you can service those that you are requesting to service. God is never going to bring something to you that you are not prepared to take care of.

God has given us people that can provide us with wisdom and direction. Use those people in your network to assist with marketing plans. Just make sure that what you say you can do you're able to accomplish. It is better to not vow than make a vow and not fulfill it. Remember, over promising and under delivering is the super fast way to go out of business.

Most people do not plan to do wrong by customers. One of the leading causes of giving poor customer service is due to putting trust in money; that leads to poor actions. Just as our money has the famous and well-known line "In God We Trust" scribed on it, that statement has to be our mantra too. In God only do we TRUST and when we are in business not only is our reputation on the line but God's reputation as well. If you have not been fair to your customers then repent, turn from your old ways and get a new way. You may have to go back and make some things right or just move forward under new management.

Customer Exercise

This exercise is designated to help you operate in faith and not foolishness with customers.

- Determine the number of customer that you can properly service

- Determine how you can give your customer more than expected service

- Determine how you will handle situations with customers when you miss the mark of exceptional service

- Determine specific time to pray for your new and current customers daily

7. Designate the Proper Entity Selection
"A house is built by wisdom
   and becomes strong through good sense"

Proverbs 24:3

You have to determine how you are going to set up your business or change the setup for your business to move to the next level. Many entrepreneurs will wake up and declare they are in business and be off to the race. We are not just entrepreneurs but Faithpreneurs that operate with Godly principles. God is a God of order and our business must be in order as well. Before you can fully begin your business you will have to determine the best legal entity selection for your organization/company. This step is vitally important! Some people will want to become Corporations, LLCs, S Corporations, Sole Proprietors, but there's not one size that fits all. It's important for you to determine the best fit for you based upon business facts. Some important considerations:

- How much are you prepared to invest?
- o Many state filing forms require fees
- Who will be your business leadership?
- o Is it just you or do you plan to have a President, Secretary and Treasurer
- o Do you plan to have shareholders?
- o Will you have partners?
- Will your business be a legacy?
- o If it's important to you to leave this business for your family, who will play a factor in the decision process and you must develop a legacy plan.
- Your willingness and ability to handle the operation paperwork and the requirements

- o Some legal entities require you to maintain board meeting minutes
- • The desired tax impact and treatment
- o Some entities require reporting on your personal return
- o Some entities require business returns to be filed prior to your individual return
- • Personal Asset protection
- o Some entities will treat you and the business as one in the same. This could increase risk exposure to your personal assets

This is why one size does not fit all. Your individual situation should be reviewed to determine the best entity classification for your company at this time. There are times that you will start off as one entity and change to another based upon the performance of your company. You have to be in touch with your business or have a power play team member that you can seek direction from. You are investing time and resources into this business and it would be terrible to lose it due to lack of planning. Remember the enemy only has three weapons: Steal, Kill, and Destroy to use against citizens of the kingdom. The failure to take care of your legal setup properly can open the doors for the enemy to be successful should you fall prey to a lawsuit, judgment or misunderstanding. The failure to do things properly doesn't just cost you time, resources and money; it could cost you your legacy.

I have provided you an entity classification chart in the resource section that can assist you in your selection of how to structure your company from a corporate standpoint. It is always recommended to seek one on one direction from someone with business experience.

Legal Entity Exercise Assignment

Review the chart comparison. Based upon the information what entity structure appears to be appropriate for your endeavor?

Success Story Highlight-The ClayGroup

1. **Person Name: Frank Clay**
2. **Company Name: The ClayGroup**
3. **Years In Business: 4**
4. **Number of Employees: 8**

5. **Business overview:** The ClayGroup is a national Service Disabled Veteran Owned Small Business (SDVOSB) that distributes brand name products and services to the federal government using an independent network of distributors that provide local deliveries and customer service. Our mission is to provide quality products and services that assist the government in maintaining cleaner, healthier, safer and greener federal facilities.

6. **How does your business relate to your God given purpose:** In the Bible, in the Book of Mathew, there is the parable of the Talents and I continually reflect on this scripture when it comes to business. God has given me the talent of being able to "take care of the business at hand" and I have always felt the responsibility of the one that was given the Five Talents. With this witness, I have seen as my God given purpose to take whatever God has given me and make it profitable for all associated with business... partners, employees, customers and the community. I believe when I am blessed with success, God is saying you have been faithful with what I have given you so I will give you more to work with, develop, create and manage.

Matthew 25:20-21

20. The man who had received the five talents brought the other five. 'Master,' he said, 'you entrusted me with five talents. See, I have gained five more.'

21. "His master replied, 'Well done, good and faithful servant! You have been faithful with a few things; I will put you in charge of many things. Come and share your master's happiness!'

7. What is your passion: My passion is bringing out the best in people and getting the best out of the opportunities given to me. I am passionate about embracing my faith, hoping for the better and seeing how God continues his faithfulness to me and blessing my work and my business. Morning by morning new mercies I see... all I need in my life and my business, God has provided...what He gives me is enough to run with... great is thy faithfulness.

Lamentations 3:21-24

21. This I recall to my mind, therefore have I hope.

22. It is of the LORD's mercies that we are not consumed, because his compassions fail not.

23. They are new every morning: great is thy faithfulness.

24. The LORD is my portion saith my soul; therefore will I hope in him.

8. What biblical principle has been part of your business: Here is some wisdom... "work hard" while you can. Anyone can make it, success and failure happen to the best of us in business so do your best and find out how God will bless your work and your business. We never know what is going to happen in business because things happen! I gleam these thoughts in the spirit from reading

Ecclesiastes 9:10-12:

10. Whatever your hand finds to do, do it with all your might, for in the grave, [c] where you are going, there is neither working nor planning nor knowledge nor wisdom.

11. I have seen something else under the sun:
The race is not to the swift
or the battle to the strong,
nor does food come to the wise
or wealth to the brilliant
or favor to the learned;
but time and chance happen to them all.

12. Moreover, no man knows when his hour will come:
As fish are caught in a cruel net,
or birds are taken in a snare,
so men are trapped by evil times
that fall unexpectedly upon them.

9. What biblical principle would you encourage any entrepreneur to engage in as part of their business principles. There is much written in the Bible about the ox and its importance to building and making things happen. In business you need an ox on your team and when they are working don't stop them, even though things may not be perfect. Respect the key players on your team. You want the increase in business.

Proverbs 14:4
4. Where no oxen are, the crib is clean: but much increase is by the strength of the ox.

10. What business principles have worked that you feel has lead to your success: Have faith in God and faith in your business...

Mark 11:22

22. And Jesus answering saith unto them, Have faith in God.

11. What do you think you should have done more of or less of that would have made your road to success easier or shorter: Nothing, experience is a great teacher. It is important to work hard at meeting each challenge of each day. Being in business and doing God's work is not easy and it is not quick. It is hard work and sacrifices are required but in the end it is rewarding if your business is profitable. You must be devoted and dedicated; you have to hang in there. Don't be weary and don't faint for your time will come. Success is near. Isaiah 40:31

But they that wait upon the LORD shall renew their strength; they shall mount up with wings as eagles; they shall run, and not be weary; and they shall walk, and not faint.

If you want to do business with the world's largest purchaser, then your customer is the US Government. This customer doesn't mind working with small businesses, however, you need to know the rules of the game. It is important to know how to search and bid for the work. You will need to be properly setup with DUNS, CAGE, GSA Schedule and certification may be needed. When it is time to collect your money then you need to be setup to accept the form of payment the government pays with.

ww.claygroupllc.com

8. Obtain Federal, State, and Local Identification Numbers

This is one of the processes that I have seen incorrectly handled numerous times. The Internal Revenue Service has made the process for obtaining an EIN or Employer Identification Number pretty easy and user friendly. They're assuming that you are seeking guidance prior to using the system or you have read the instruction booklet. Many opt to set up their business themselves and obtain the identification number without knowing the responsibility that comes with the number.

The identification number should be matched to your legal setup. If you are going to be a corporation then that should be properly marked during the identification number process. I have seen clients that intended to be taxed as an LLC receive an EIN that causes them to be taxed incorrectly and ended up communicating incorrectly. The incorrect communications causes them to be taxed as a sole proprietor. The errors are often not caught until the next year so they are now faced with tax, payroll and filing issues.

All businesses are not required to have identification numbers. If you are going to have employees, setup bank accounts, obtain certification, obtain funding and/or be setup as a certain legal entity then you may be required to have federal, state, and local identification numbers. You can obtain a copy of the actual Internal Revenue Service forms on our website (www.fivestartaxkc.com). The most important thing to remember from this section is that you may have certain filing requirements once you obtain these identification numbers. If you indicated that you were going to hire employees then you will be expected to file payroll tax forms. Just because you decided not to hire any employees doesn't change the filing requirement. Some agencies will require you to file zero returns and failure to do so could cost you your professional license or you could be accessed estimated taxes. It is always best to understand what you are doing before you pull the trigger. Most issues can be fixed but it may cost you and require someone else to fix it.

9. Create an Accounting Process

"Do not use dishonest standards when measuring length, weight, or volume.[36] Your scales and weights must be accurate. Your containers for measuring dry materials or liquids must be accurate.[a] I am the LORD your God who brought you out of the land of Egypt."

Leviticus 19:35-36

You must have a systematic approach to record the daily transactions of your business. An accounting system is any system that will allow you to record those transactions and recall them to produce reports or answer questions. The system can be a computerized software system that is purchased from any office supply store. If you are unfamiliar with them, a very popular computerized software is QuickBooks which is produced by Intuit. Many of my consultation clients find it user friendly. The question is not the software but the user of the software. If your transactions are put in incorrectly then your system will produce incorrect reports and answers.

You do not have to become an Accountant but you need to know and understand your business. Even if you are going to hire an Accountant, you need to be able to determine if the accountant is effective or if they specialize in your industry. Some things to consider before hiring an Accountant:

• Qualifications: Certified Public Accountant (CPA) designation does not mean they can do it all. Some CPA's work in a specific field of accounting, like audit or tax. They may be strong in tax but weak in financial reporting. A CPA may or may not be right for you. They typically charge a higher hourly fee for services provided than a degreed accountant. Degreed accountants may be better suited for you than a CPA. Look at the qualifications for what you need them to accomplish and then decide.

• Communication Skills: They can be one of the best accountants in the world, but if they cannot listen to your request and explain information in a manner that you can understand, then they are not good for you at all. You have to understand the direction your Accountant will give you. Remember that some Accountants prefer to work with numbers and not people so communication skills may be lacking. Keep searching until you find the right fit.

• Specialization: Accounting is a wide field and nobody can be strong in all the areas of accounting. Accountants tend to have a strong suite and you should identify what their weakness is so you can staff your team properly.

• Scope of Services: What do you need them to do? Do you need them for tax returns, financial statements, investments, software selection/training, or consulting? Make sure you know what you want because this is exactly what you may get. Additional services typically elicit additional fees, so never assume they are covering everything just because you paid them for a tax return.

• Relationship Factor: An accountant relationship should be considered long-term. The longer you work with someone should allow them to better serve you because they have historical information, it would help to be equally yoked in this process to. If you are extending your faith for this business and this person is handling your financial affairs it would be great to have the power of agreement. The relationship can work whether they believe in the manner you do or not but be prepared if they provide you natural advice that may not line up with your spiritual direction. For example, if a part of your company isn't performing well and they advise you to sell but you feel an undeniable unction to keep it. Your motivation should not be just about money but also the ability to increase the Kingdom of God. Will they be ok seeing you give 30% of your gross revenue out in charitable contributions?

Success Story Highlight-Lamp Glow Industries, Inc

1. **Person Name: Vern Haynes, EE, MBA, President/CEO**
2. **Company Name: Lamp Glow Industries, Inc.**
3. **Years In Business: 32 Years**
4. **Number of Employee: 5**
5. **Business overview:**

Lamp Glow Industries has made significant progress over the past 32 years in its business development efforts for renewable energy and ancillary components in the African, Caribbean, Central and South America Regions. Our knowledge of the market is extensive and we are currently developing a multi-faceted aggressive marketing campaign built on this foundation.

Access to electrical power is one of the primary driving forces of a modern society. It dramatically affects the way we work, the way we play and ultimately the way we live. Electrical power and clean, safe water enhances the quality of life, can create a greater sense of security for our homes, schools, hospitals, and businesses and enables efficiencies otherwise unattainable. Dependence on that power is the price we pay for its many benefits. As a safe, clean, quiet, reliable and affordable source of energy, our Smart-PowerSystems are available to address the critical electrical demands needed to operate the various facilities throughout the world.

Recognizing the high cost of energy in these Regions, there are advantages that accrue by merging proven water purification and wastewater treatment with renewable energy technology.

Lamp Glow Industries has operated successfully under the concept of "Strategic Alliance Partners" which we define as "Organized cooperation between independent companies and institutions having complimentary technology, expertise and market focus in the renewable energy, water purification and wastewater treatment business and related technologies, who are philosophically attuned and directed towards strategic goals that are advantageous to the members of the alliance and the customer".

We have combined our resources to provide Turnkey Solutions, modular systems utilizing the "Plug and Play" concept for ease of installation at an affordable price. Further, we offer Maintenance and Training Programs, which make the user self-sufficient with sustainable technology for the near term as well as the long term and create jobs in the community.

6. How does your business relate to your God given purpose: Lamp Glow Industries, Inc. was founded on the biblical Psalm 119:105: "Thy word is a lamp unto my feet and a light unto my path". Hence, being able to provide vision and illumination and help to those in need.

7. What is your passion: Helping others who are unable to help themselves through modern technologies.

8. What biblical principle has been part of your business: Proverbs 24:3-4 "An enterprise that is built by wise planning becomes strong through common sense and profits wonderfully by keeping abreast of the facts".

9. What biblical principle would you encourage any entrepreneur to engage in as part of their business principles: The Joseph and Joshua Strategic Planning Principles: Seek Godly wisdom; ask Him for knowledge and spiritual discernment.

1. Preparation – Be prepared, take nothing for granted, know your strengths and weaknesses
2. Positioning – Know your market niche and not be everything to everyone
3. Posturing – People must come to you because you have what they need
4. Portals – Look for unusual channels to move through to seize the opportunity

10. What business principle have worked that you feel has lead to your success: I will find a way or make a way and I will not be denied!

11. What do you think you should have done more of or less of that would have made your road to success easier or shorter: Life is a journey and there are no short cuts. Trying to second guess anything is mere hind-sight and hind-sight is always 20-20. We should learn from our mistakes and grow stronger in the process as we face these challenges head on... there are no guarantees to success in life.

"What lies behind us and what lies before us are small matters compared to what lies within us".

Ralph Waldo Emerson

10. Resolve Funding Requirement and Options

"But don't begin until you count the cost. For who would begin construction of a building without first calculating the cost to see if there is enough money to finish it? 29 Otherwise, you might complete only the foundation before running out of money, and then everyone would laugh at you. 30 They would say, 'There's the person who started that building and couldn't afford to finish it!'

Luke 14:28-30

How will you deal with the money? It's as simple as a decision; just as the tithing off of Gross vs. Net is a decision, determining your funding options is another important decision. I have consulted with Faithpreneurs that started their business with no loans. They started the business with their own personal money and took a debt free position (this is known as bootstrapping). Also, I have consulted with Faithpreneurs that have obtained loans and dealt with investors. The success or failure of those businesses was not because of the decision to get into debt or not. The success was in the businesses ability to make an objective decision and determine how the decision will impact the business from a natural perspective. Some of them started off as home-based businesses based upon their lending objectives. You counted the cost in the Action Plan section of your business plan summary or Go/NO Go form. You wrote the vision to make it plain upon the table. Your lending objectives could alter those plans. If you are not open to getting a loan and your revenue cannot support an employee then you have to plan to do most of the work or extend your faith to generate enough revenue to support that employee that is expecting to be paid.

Bad credit can close the door to lending options; however those credit issues should be addressed. Credit is not less important because you are not seeking lending. Your credit can impact your business' ability to obtain bonding insurance, vendors, or supplies. If credit is an issue, then institute a plan to fix the issues.

Faith and foolishness are two different things. If God tells you something and you believe it... then it is settled. However, do not put God in foolishness for the world to think that God is flakey, when it really is you. You cannot expect the bank to lend you a million dollars for a startup with bad credit. That is foolishness not faith. Don't get caught up with foolish things such as lending out money. A person that has bad credit flat out knows the reason why. Whatever the reasons may be for having a track record of not paying bills on time or not paying them at all, your credit score is really a reflection of how truthful you are with lenders. Christians should not have bad credit, that shows that we borrow, make a promise to pay back the money, and then go back on our word. I beg you to rectify your credit. Your self esteem will rise and your ability for more opportunities when you need them.

Let's flip the coin for a minute. The word is very clear about the believer being the lender and not the borrower. Extending credit to your customers can be the "destroy weapon" in action. If too many of your customers obtain your product/service without paying then you could be allowing them to run you out of business. Don't get me wrong, it is okay to use "Freemium" to launch but you must make sure that people know that the work you've put in is valuable and worth payment. Don't be afraid or feel guilty for charging for your businesses services. Look at it this way, your customers willingly go to the supermarket and give every manufacturer what they ask, why is it any different for you? You have come too far to end it because you cannot say "NO". If you feel that free is what you must do, don't be afraid to be creative. If you give away your services require 10-20 referral leads that you can follow up with. If you do something like this, make sure your customer pre-qualifies them for you by having them send out a testimonial e-mail and letting those leads know to look out for your business.

Take time to meditate on your business, various ideas, and ways to bless people and you in turn be blessed also. Ideas will flow. Remember, Jesus was deliberate in everything that he did. You do the same. If you carefully read the scriptures you will see that Jesus was calculated, deliberate and could flow with the situation in front of him. If it was good enough for God , it's good enough for you! Now let's look at your lending objectives:

Lending Objective

Pray and seek God for direction regarding your lending position in your business . Write it down.

I believe that God is directing me to

_____

_____

_____

_____

_____

_____

_____

_____

_____

_____

_____

_____

_____

11. Render unto Caesar and God
those things that belong to them

"Well then," he said, "give to Caesar what belongs to Caesar, and give to
God what belongs to God."

Luke 20:25

Your greatest business strategy as a Faithpreneur is your ability to be a constant supply station for the Kingdom of God. Your business can not rob God and expect for it to be well. Your business must release the tithe. The tithe is the part of the whole that belongs to God, 10%. Some of my Faithpreneur consultation clients have asked do I pay the 10% off the Gross or the net revenue. There are two different viewpoints and I encourage you to consult with your spiritual mentor or Pastor. The Gross Revenue is the money that comes into the door before expenses. The Net Income is the Gross Revenue less business expenses. Some businesses have a loss for three years, so if the Faithpreneur viewpoint is to tithe off of the net then they would not have anything to tithe off of. The one thing that I would say is be consistent in whatever you decide to do. If it is the gross that you choose then it is the gross on $100.00 month or $1,000,000 year, it doesn't deviate. Do not allow the enemy to disqualify you because of 10%. That 10% is the confident assurance that you can boldly pray and command increase to come into your business. You can boldly rebuke lack off of your business and employees. You can call forth supernatural favor in business deals. Do not mess with your confident assurance.

You may be saying "I get the tithing part and I already do, what about my offering?" The offering is the condition of the Faithpreneur heart. The tithe is obedience and the offering is the sacrifice. That is the seed that you are willing to plant based upon direction from the voice of God. Your seed planting may be to provide scholarships for kids to obtain higher education. Your seed planting may be to support organizations that God told you to financially support. The ground you sow into needs to be directed by God and then it will be your "Good Ground." When you plant into good ground then you will reap a harvest. Your harvest may be your ability to hire when others are firing. Your harvest may be supernatural favor with influential people. Your harvest may be your ability to provide the best quality service in the most efficient manner; so much, that nobody can understand how your team can do it so easily with low to minimal stress. Your harvest may be experience increases in a down economy.

My mentor, Dr. Donna Houpe frequently says, "Understand that you have to sow to where you want to go." Some of your sowing may not be just money but resources. You may have the resources or ability that an organization needs. Your sowing of that resource or ability may be the very thing that opens the door for promotion to the next level of business growth. It can be easy to slide into manipulation so keep your motives pure and do NOT expect to reap where you sow and all will be well. I am not saying that you will NOT reap from where you sow but if you do not EXPECT it then you will not be tempted to do things for desired outcomes; this practice will also keep you open to the voice of the Lord. You will have to trust God to bring your reaping partner to the table.

There are entrepreneurs that are NOT Faithpreneurs that used the sowing and reaping law. This law is like gravity, it works no matter what your beliefs may be.

Most true believers will not knowingly want to rob God but Caesar could be the little fox. Do not let the little foxes, like Income Taxes, ruin the vein. One of the top reasons that businesses fail is failure to file and pay income tax returns. Tax professionals have a saying that one of the easiest loans you can get is one that you do not have to apply or qualify for. The tax payment that should be set aside is not your money so you are using "Uncle Sam's" money. This is a costly game to play that always ends in high penalties, interest, or an out of business sign.

If you have tax problems, ignoring the letters, notices, or calls will not make it go away. You can't faith it away either (remember that faith is not flakey either). Just like the procrastinator had to take the first step towards action, you must do the same and GET help. Once you have done what is required then you can repent and ask God for grace and mercy.

"To whom much is given then much is also required" so if this Faithpreneur endeavor is going to be fruitful, then you have to plan to pay taxes.

Sowing Assignment

Pray and seek God's direction for organizations that you plan to support. What amount do you desire to give away to that organization within next 12 months?

Write out a check to the organization for that amount and keep it before you to build your faith.

© Trevor Logan 2010

12. Think Big!
"Now all glory to God, who is able, through his mighty power at work within us, to accomplish infinitely more than we might ask or think"

Ephesians 3:20

Once you have sought God's direction for your purpose, timing, power team, and you have acted on it by creating the plans, using godly principals, and business systems then you might as well THINK BIG. If you are going to dream then super size your dream. Believe God for the impossible. Many have done what you are dreaming of doing and many have accomplished greatness. Read about those people that have done the great. Study those individuals that are at the level that you desire from God. Find people that pull the best out of you, listen to CD's that motivate you, watch movies that you can pull principals out of that cause you to grow. You need your "game song or power statement"; which is the saying that causes your insides to stir up when you say it or hear it. Do you feel compelled to take the next step? Push yourself to achieve greatness. Push others to achieve their greatness. Enjoy the journey that you are taking during the process. Every day is a gift from God so you might as well enjoy the present that you received.

Don't forget that sometimes God doesn't reveal the ending to us at the beginning, because our character isn't ready for it. God will never give you something that is going to destroy you so make the character adjustments as required. If you fail at something then be quick to repent and get back up and move forward. You only fail if you STOP. Never quit and never stop looking for the "gate" of opportunity/direction. The economy and season will produce gates of opportunity.

Faithpreneurship may require you to make hard decisions in a quick manner. Remember you have insider information so you are never alone in the process if you are willing to stay in constant communication with your manufacturer, Jesus Christ. Your communication is prayer, fasting, reading the word of God, and meditation on the Word. God can do anything but fail. He is looking for willing vessels that will believe the impossible, work the principles, and make the Kingdom of God the primary focus.

Think Big Exercise Assignment

If things should get rocky what song or phrase can you play or say to get you back in the game?

_____

_____

_____

_____

_____

_____

_____

_____

Resource Section

Forms, Charts & Check list Attached
• *Legal Entity Comparison Chart*
• *Go/No Go Form*
• *Business Plan Checklist*

Recommend List of other Readings or Listening
• CD: Our Helper: The Person of the Holy Spirit
  Dr. Steve Houpe
• CD: In Pursuit of the Mission: Becoming the Person God
  has Called you to be - Dr. Steve Houpe
• CD: It's Your Time - Dr. Steve Houpe
• Book: Prayer, Fasting, & The Anointing - Dr. Steve Houpe
• Book: Reposition Yourself - Bishop T.D. Jakes
• Book: The Law of Confession - Dr. Bill Winston
• Book: Kings and Priest - Dr. Bill Winston
• Book: The Road to Someplace Better
  Lillian Lincoln Lambert
• Book: Connect & Grown Rich - Rob Coats
• Book: The Millionaire Ex-Convict - Uchendi Nwani
• Book: Becoming a Person of Influence - John Maxwell
• Book: The E Myth Revisited - Michael E. Gerber

Recommend List of Resources for Research
• *New Living Translation Bible version*
• *www.sba.gov*
• *www.business.gov*
• *www.score.org*
• *www.irs.gov*
• *www.annualcreditreport.com*

[i]*All scriptures are taken from the New Living Translation Bible version*

Business Entity Comparison Chart

Comparison Factors	Sole Proprietorship (SP)	General Partnership (GP)
Business Formation	City tax license may be required.	No state filing required. Some states allow GP's to file at state agency. An Agreement between two or more parties. Partnership agreement should be created
Size	One person ownership	Two or more person ownership
Length of Existence	Sole proprietorship either ceases doing business or dies	Depending upon partnership agreement. Typically death or withdrawal of a partner dissolves the GP
Liability	SP has unlimited liability and can lose personal assets	General Partners are equally liable or less the partnership agreement states otherwise
Operational Procedures	Easiest with few legal requirements	Typically GP's have few legal requirements
Start up cost	Cost of business tax license	Cost of business tax license

One of the most frequently asked question we hear is, "Which business entity is right for my business?" Although we cannot give you legal advice and make that decision for you, we can offer you valuable information so you can make an informed decision based on your business needs.

Limited Liability Company (LLC)	S Corporation (S Corp)	C Corporation General Stock (C Corp)
Required to file formation document with the State filing agency. Most states require an Operating Agreement	Required to file formation document with the State filing agency. Most states require annual meetings and bylaws. Must elect S status through the IRS, additional filing required	Required to file formation document with the State filing agency. Most states require annual meetings and bylaws
Most states allow single member LLC's but some require 2 or more members	Up to 75 members/ shareholders	Unlimited
Some states allow LLC's to have a perpetual existence. Others depend upon the state's requirements	Perpetual	Perpetual
Members are not liable for debts accrued by the company or less a member secured the debt with a personal asset	Shareholders are typically not liable for the debts of the corporation. Some officers can be held liable if there is fraud or severe mismanagement.	Shareholders are typically not liable for the debts of the corporation. Some officers can be held liable if there is fraud or severe mismanagement.
Most states have some formal requirements like annual reports but are typically less than a corporation	Annual meetings, filings, and reporting required. Board of Directors and Officers must be maintained.	Annual meetings, filings, and reporting required. Board of Directors and Officers must be maintained.
State filing fee is required.	State filing fee is required.	State filing fee is required.

Business Entity Comparison Chart (Cont.)

Comparison Factors	Sole Proprietorship (SP)	General Partnership (GP)
Management	SP is in complete control of managing operations	Or less the partnership agreement states otherwise, each partner has equal management authority
Taxation	Taxed Once	Taxed Once
Pass through taxation for both income and loss	Yes	Yes
Interest Transferability	No. Or less business is sold to another party	No.
Raising Capital	Hard to get outside capital. Owner typically contributes all funds	Partners contribute capital and more capital can be raised by adding new partners
Dissolution	Easiest	Easy
Examples	Mom & Pop Ice cream shop	Land Developer

Limited Liability Company (LLC)	S Corporation (S Corp)	C Corporation General Stock (C Corp)
Management is outlined in the LLC's Operating Agreement.	Officers manage day to day corporate activities. Directors manage the officers and the overall company. Directors are elected and therefore managed by the shareholders.	ement is outlined in the LLC's Operating Agreement.
Taxed Once	Taxed Once	Double; both the corporation and shareholders are taxed
Yes	Yes	No
Depends upon the operating agreement	Yes. Some IRS regulations on stock ownership	Shares of stock are easily transferred
Some operating agreements allow interests to be sold	S Corps can sell stock to raise capital	C Corps can sell stock to raise capital
Complex. Requires filing dissolution document with state filing agency. Some states require a tax clearance prior to dissolution.	Most Complex. Requires filing dissolution document with state filing agency. Some states require a tax clearance prior to dissolution.	Most Complex. Requires filing dissolution document with state filing agency. Some states require a tax clearance prior to dissolution.
Real Estate Investment Property. Motion Picture. Any type of business depending upon specific state restrictions.	Small business or Family business such as a print shop, Pizza Parlor, or Interior Design.	Public Corporation. Software company, telecommunications company, etc.

Sample Go No Go Decision Criteria

Criteria	Yes	No	Don't Know	Points
Is your immediate family in agreement with you going into business?	+	-	-	
Is this business in your area of expertise?	+	-	-	
Have you identified your target market?	+	-	-	
Have you met or corresponded with someone that is currently in this field?	+	-	-	
Have you identified your Unique Selling position?	+	-	-	
Will this business provide you the salary to maintain your personal commitment?	+	-	-	
Have you adjusted your personal expense to free up cash flow that can be reinvested into the business?	+	-	-	
Do you feel that you have a good understanding of your industry?	+	-	-	
Have you prepared a SWOT analysis?	+	-	-	
Have you created a business plan?	+	-	-	
Have you detailed the steps required to generate projected income for year one?	+	-	-	
Are you prepared to invest required time to this business?	+	-	-	
Add one point for each +				
Subtract one point for each -				
10-12 POINTS You are ready to GO				
6-9 POINTS Keep working your plan				
0-5 POINTS- Rework your plan				

Business Plan Checklist

The following is a listing of supporting documentation that will be helpful in preparing your business plan. Also below there is a preliminary listing of questions that will ensure that your business plan is an organized, comprehensive and concise blue-print for investment opportunities and future success. You (client) will provide all supporting documentation and assist with answering key questions.

Supporting Documentation	Key Questions the business plan will need to answer.
1. Company Structure a. Brief description of the company b. Products or services listing c. List of Assets	**1. Company Structure** a. What stage is your business in? (concept, development, later stages) b. How is your business unique or what sets it apart? c. Why is this venture a good risk? d. What type of opportunity is this? (new, expansion, part-time, year-round, seasonal) e. What is your current timeline? f. Have you set your objectives?
2. Organizational Structure a. Current Organization charts b. Position descriptions c. Key employee resumes d. Personnel policies and procedures documents (if available)	**2. Organizational Structure** a. Who will manage the business? b. What are management's qualifications? c. Number of employees needed? d. How will you structure your organization? e. What are you plans for compensation? f. What licenses or permits will be needed?

Supporting Documentation	Key Questions the business plan will need to answer.
3. Financial Data a. Current budget b. Year to date financial numbers c. Monthly financial statements	**3. Financial Questions** a. What is your total estimated business income for the first year by month? b. What will your personal monthly financial needs be by month? c. What sales volume will you need in order to make a profit during the first three years? d. What are your total financial needs? e. What are your potential funding sources? What is the disbursement plan? f. How will the loans be secured?
4. Legal Authority and Structure a. Current contracts (Products or services) b. Ordinances governing your type of business	**4. Legal Authority and structure** a. What legal form of ownership will you choose and why? (ie: LLC, Sole Proprietorship, Corporation) b. What licenses or permits will you need?
5. Marketing a. Current brochures or ads	**5. Marketing Questions** a. Who are your potential customers? b. Why do customers need your product or service? c. How will you price the product or service? d. Who are your competitors? e. How are your competitors businesses positioned? f. What is your competitive advantage? g. What advertising and promotional strategies will you use?

Proverbs 20:7 (King James Version)

The just man walketh in his integrity:
his children are blessed after him.

In memory of the man that reared me in the
direction that I am walking: James C. Muse, Jr.

December 9 1949-April 4 2011

Chef Jim Muse: Creator of "Purple Pride BBQ Sauce"-

His memory and legacy will live on!

About the Author
Marquita Miller

Marquita Miller currently lives in Kansas City, Missouri. She obtained her MBA from the Keller Graduate School of Mgmt. She obtained her Bachelors' of Science (Accounting/Mgmt) from Park University. She is the owner and operator of Five Star Tax & Business Solutions headquarters in Kansas City, Missouri. During her tenure working as an accountant for Fortune 500 companies then she launched the business as a part-time hobby in 2000. Marquita identified early on that her target market would be start-ups to medium sized organizations so she resigned from her ideal career ladder position to work for smaller organizations to gain more practical experience for that market. In 2005 she put feet to faith and entered the world of entrepreneurship on a full-time basis. That would prove to be a providential moment that would lead to Marquita and her company being ranked as one of Kansas City, Missouri's Rising Stars of the Year. It also lead to other business acknowledgements like; Small Business of the Year nominee, obtaining certifications such as Women owned/Minority owned business. Marquita has also been able to hire team members to assist with carry out the vision and currently developing affiliated locations throughout the United States.

All of this has been accomplished while holding titles of wife, mother, daughter, mentor, women of God, active leader in her church, educator, speaker, radio show host, and board member to several organizations. She has seemed to stretch the limits of time and made her latest mark by completing her first book.

To contact Marquita Miller for book signings, speaking engagements or to order more copies of this book-send an E-mail to **info@fivestartaxkc.com** or visit the we*bsite at* **www.fivestartaxkc.com**

Services of Five Star Tax & Business Solutions, LLC

Five Star Tax & Business Solutions
provides the following services:

- Tax Planning (Individuals & Businesses)
- Tax Preparation(Individuals & Businesses)
- Full Service Accounting Services
- Payroll
- Business Startup
- Business performance consulting
- Revenue Generations Consulting
- Financial Planning
- Resource provide to large network of service/product providers

Contact Information for Highlight Success Stories

Company Name	Owner	Product/Service	Contact Info
Uchendi Nwani Enterprise	Uchendi (Chin) Nwani	• Author of Millionaire Ex-Convict • Founder: Nwani's Barber & Styles • Founder: International Barber & Style College	Email: 1chin@comcast.net Address: 3744 Annex Avenue Suite A 2 Website: www.2ibs.org www.1chin.com
Frank Clay	The Leander Group	• President of Leander Group • Business Consultant	Website: leandergroup.org
Tarsha Polk	The Marketing Lady	• Radio Show Host • Business Coaching • Marketing Consultant • Public Speaker	Website: themarketinglady.com
Vern Haynes	Lamp Glow Industries, Inc	• President of Lamp Glow Industries, Inc.	Email: veh79@earthlink.net Website: smart-powersystems.com

Notes

Notes

Notes

Notes

Notes

Notes